What the Bible
REALLY
Says about Prosperity

RICHARD ROBERTS

Unless otherwise indicated, all Scripture quotations are paraphrased from the New King James Version of the Bible.

Copyright © 2019

by Richard Roberts

Tulsa, Oklahoma

Printed in the United States of America

All rights reserved

ISBN 978-1-7325385-5-9

What the Bible REALLY Says about Prosperity

by Richard Roberts

My wife Lindsay and I were in a Southwest Believer's Convention in Fort Worth, Texas, and during one of the services, Kenneth Copeland called us up to the front and began to prophesy over us.

One of the things he said was that there was a new anointing coming on me to teach on the laws of prosperity.

Since that night, I have been studying on

prosperity from the Bible's perspective…not from the way the world looks at prosperity, but from the way God looks at prosperity. The Lord has moved on my heart and given me a message.

It's a message that is so critical to our lives and to how we think about *who God is* and *how He operates*…whether we see Him as a stingy, selfish God, or as a lavish, giving Father. ***If I could change something about the way some people believe, I would do my best to help them understand: God wants YOU to prosper!***

The Truth Regarding Biblical Prosperity

I've never accepted the world's idea of a "prosperity gospel," but I want you to know that I do sincerely believe in Bible prosperity—the kind of prosperity God talks about in His Word.

And, let me tell you, God talked a lot about prosperity in His Word! So, God must have thought that knowing His principles concerning prosperity would be of great importance in our lives. However, nowhere in the Bible is a *prosperity gospel* mentioned or taught.

The term "prosperity gospel" and the teaching surrounding it was created by men…not God. Men, and women, have taken God's Word out of context and used it to try to manipulate people into believing that if you give a certain amount of money, you can receive a miracle from God. That kind of teaching is in error and it is not scriptural.

However, I wholeheartedly endorse Bible prosperity.

Scripture clearly indicates that God Himself delights in the prosperity of His people (Psalm 35:27) and that it's His highest wish that we prosper and be in health, even as our soul prospers (3 John 2). God wants us to prosper—in fact, to *thrive*—in every area of our lives. That includes our spirit, mind, body and emotions. That includes thriving in our relationship with God, and with others. And it also includes thriving in our finances.

The true message of biblical prosperity has to do with discovering and becoming acquainted with God's ways of doing and being, and then emulating those ways of doing and being in our own lives. The problems arise because of not knowing God's ways of doing things and in not knowing what God's Word has to say about prospering in Him. We've all tried it the world's way, and the world's way does not work!

I heard Kenneth Copeland say, "The world's

shortages have no effect on someone who's already in heaven. Therefore, they should have no effect on those of us who have made Jesus the Lord of our lives in the here and now."

When we asked Jesus into our lives and confessed Him as Lord and Savior, our spirit-man was reborn and we were brought into fellowship with God, thereby putting us into a position to receive, by faith, everything that Jesus did for us on the Cross. Jesus redeemed us from our sin, and He paid the price for our healing, peace, and prosperity (Isaiah 53:5).

God wants us to experience the joy of having our prayers answered and our needs met. In John 16:24, Jesus said, *Until now you have asked nothing in My name. Ask, and you will receive, that your joy may be full.* And in John 15:7, Jesus gave us this promise, *If you abide in Me, and My words abide in you, you will ask what you desire, and it shall be done for you.*

The question we have to ask ourselves is, are we abiding (living) in, and for, God? Are we allowing His Word to live in and through us?

Prayer and Faith... They Go Hand-in-Hand

This God-kind of living and loving that I'm talking about is called "seed-faith living." It's not about some man-made theory. I'm talking about a prayer way of life...of calling those things that are not as though they are...and believing them in by faith.

God began to talk to us about prospering in the very first book of the Bible. In Genesis chapter 8, verse 26, He says, *"While the earth remains, seedtime and harvest will not cease."*

You see, it's a scientific and biological fact

that everything in life comes from a seed. You and I came from a seed and without it, we wouldn't be here. And as every farmer knows, you have to plant seed first before you can expect a harvest. A farmer would look pretty silly if he went out into his field to gather a harvest when he had failed to plant the seeds! *First* comes the seed, and *then* comes the harvest or the increase. It's one of God's natural laws. The cycle of sowing and reaping, of giving and receiving, will never end. Harvest time will always follow seed planting.

Sowing seed is about the giving of ourselves and planting good seeds—our time, our talents, our resources—into the lives of others and into the work of the kingdom of God. This kind of living (and giving) also positions us to receive all that God has for us as we walk out His plan for our lives. And we can rest assured that God's plans for us are good plans for our benefit and not for harm (Jeremiah 29:11).

It's also important to point out that God's view of prosperity is about much more than just having money.

When people who are not born again think of physical and financial prosperity, they most often think of gold and silver, financial favor, power, or political and social favor. And when they think of mental prosperity, they believe it is only head knowledge.

But let me assure you… Wealth, power, and knowledge alone cannot solve every problem. And money makes a lousy god. It can't buy good health or prevent sickness and disease.

It's like my dad, Oral Roberts, used to say… "Any old dead fish can float downstream, but it takes a live fish to swim upstream." Swimming upstream goes against what the world has taught us about what it means to prosper. It's going God's way, under His direction—doing what He wants us to do—that will make all the difference.

Is It All about Money?

In 3 John 2, when God says, *Beloved, I pray that you may prosper in all things and be in health, just as your soul prospers,* He's talking about having "all things" in our lives being healthy and prosperous and lining up with His Word and His will. As we receive wisdom and revelation from the Holy Spirit (Ephesians 1:17) and get to know Jesus and His ways better, everything in our lives—spiritually, mentally, physically and financially—are to mature and increase, just as our soul (our mind, will, and emotions) matures and grows.

Yes, our finances are a part of it. God knows that we live in a society where we have to have money to live—to pay our bills, to help others, and to further the Gospel message. He wants us to enjoy the life He's given us. And that includes spending our money on things that bring us happiness. ***Money, in and of itself, is not evil. It's the love of money*** which is at the root of all kinds of evil (1 Timothy 6:10).

There is also some reverse teaching, and beliefs out there on being prosperous which are not scriptural. Many people believe and teach that being prosperous is wrong and that in order to serve God, you must be poor and have nothing. Well, according to the Word of God, that suggestion is completely wrong! If prosperity is evil, why would God tell us it's His highest wish for us that we prosper and be in health?

I did some studying on some of the "buzz words" we always hear when it comes to the subject of prosperity. Let's look at a couple of them…

The word "prosper" means to favor, to render successful, to succeed.

Then there's the word I used earlier… "thrive." To thrive means to be fortunate or prosperous, to grow and to increase. It also means to fly high and to flourish, to make steady progress. God intends for you to always be moving forward in Him and not to be in a state of lack or of not having your basic needs met.

The opposite of God's ways of prospering and thriving means to decline, to become smaller, to decrease… a gradual and continuous loss of strength. Now, I don't know about you, but I don't like these descriptions and I don't want to go the opposite way. I want to go God's way!

What about Tithing... Is It Still for Today?

Another erroneous teaching out there says that since we live under the New Covenant after Jesus died on the Cross and rose again, the teaching about tithing in the Old Testament does not need to be followed.

Well, part of that statement is true. Those who have accepted Jesus' sacrifice on the Cross and who have asked Him into their hearts do live under the New Covenant. Believers will not be judged under the law, but by grace. However, Jesus did not come to do away with the law and the prophets. He came to fulfill them.

In the Old Testament, in the book of Genesis, we learn that Abraham, whom God blessed and made "the father of many nations," was not always a believer. While Abraham was still a pagan, he heard God's voice when God spoke to him and told him to leave his family and travel to a place which He would set before him. Now, Abraham didn't know where God was leading him, but He obeyed. And when he arrived, God had brought Abraham to the land that later became Israel. And God began to prosper Abraham in that land. *Abram acquired sheep and cattle, male and female donkeys, male and female servants, and camels* (Genesis 12:16). In fact, Abraham prospered so much that he became the richest man in that part of the world at that time.

Over time, and through many experiences with God, Abraham began to understand that the One who had spoken to him and guided him to this new land and prospered him was *the Most High God, the possessor of heaven and earth; the one who delivered him from all his enemies.* And when that realization came to him, he wanted to honor God. So he began to give a "tithe" or a tenth of all that he had to Melchizedek, the priest of Salem. (The word tithe literally means increase.) Abraham gave a tithe, or a tenth, of all his increase to honor God.

But after a while, Abraham began to get into fear and worry about what he was giving to God.

And you know, that can happen with us, too. We can feel the leading of the Lord to give into His work and then we're reminded about this bill or that bill, or the children's braces we have to pay for, or the college tuition we need to save for…or whatever the need might be. And we can sometimes become fearful and begin to withhold from God.

But know this… Every time we sow a seed of our faith, the devil will try to come in and stop our seed from working for us. He'll try to make us doubt God's promises, to doubt His provision and His love for us as His children. Satan doesn't want us to prosper and to be able to tell of God's goodness or to have the resources to help others or to give to further God's kingdom. But remember, God can only use and multiply, or increase, what we release into His hands.

God came again to Abraham and said, *"Do not be afraid. I am your shield. I am your exceeding great reward"* (Genesis 15:1).

I believe God would say that same thing to us, today. **"Don't be afraid! I am your shield. Look to Me as your Source."** We can put our faith in God and in His Word and trust that He will bring into our lives the miracle harvest we've been praying for. He is the author and finisher of our faith (Hebrews 12:2) and He is a rewarder of those who diligently seek Him

(Hebrews 11:6).

When you sow or give to God, in faith, you have a Bible right to expect a return or a harvest of blessing from Him. It's not a sin to expect a return from God. His Word says, *Whatever a man sows, that will he also reap* (Galatians 6:7). When you give your best—an acceptable and well-pleasing sacrifice which is attached to your faith (Philippians 4:18)—you have a Bible right to expect God's best in return.

But in whose life does the promise of "God's best" come to pass? His promises come to those who have made up their mind that they are going to serve God and obey His Word…that they are going to pray and use their faith when they sow their seeds. The multiplied harvest, according to God's Word in Mark 11:23-24, is going to come to those who sow their seed in good soil, believe God, and are looking for and expecting miracles in their lives!

Living Life "from the Inside Out"

Living in expectation of God's goodness is what my wife, Lindsay, likes to call "living from the inside out."

When I was only five years old, my dad, who was a golfer, put a golf club in my hand and began to teach me how to play. He made me stand right, he made me hold the club right, he made me swing the right way, and he taught me that you have to swing "from the inside out."

At first, I didn't understand it. But he demonstrated that swinging from the inside out produces a straight ball flight. "If you swing from the outside in," my dad said, "the ball is struck with side spin, which forces the ball to go to the right, losing distance and direction." My dad taught me that you have to swing from the inside out when playing golf. And he also taught me, that's how you have to live your life too… from the inside out. It may not always be the easiest way or the most comfortable, but it will be the straight and narrow way which leads to LIFE. (See Matthew 7:14.)

Opening the Windows of Heaven

Did you know that a person can steal from God?

No, we can't reach up into heaven and physically take something from God, but we *can* rob Him of the opportunity to bless us and to provide for us. So many Christians today who do not tithe and do not give to the Lord, who don't keep His Word, are wondering why they are in the condition they're in.

God sent the prophet Malachi to the nation of Israel to prophesy to them because they had forgotten God's goodness and had taken it for granted. Their worship and praise of Him had grown cold and they had stopped sowing and giving unto God. As a result, they began to have many problems. Malachi spoke the word of the Lord to them…

"Will a man rob God? Yet you have robbed Me! But you say, 'In what way have we robbed You?' In tithes and offerings. You are cursed with a curse, for you have robbed Me, even this whole nation. Bring all the tithes into the storehouse, that there may be food in My house, and try Me now in this," says the Lord of hosts, *"if I will not open for you the windows of heaven and pour out for you such blessing that there will not be room enough to receive it. And I will rebuke the devourer for your sakes"* (Malachi 3:8-11).

I believe it's worth mentioning that only twice

in the Bible does God use the phrase "the windows of heaven." The first time was in the days of Noah, a time of destruction upon mankind when the windows of heaven were opened and the earth endured a great flood of water for 40 days and 40 nights. But in this second and only other time, in Malachi 3, God said He would open the windows of heaven to "pour out a blessing."

So, let's examine these verses further…
What, or where, is the storehouse? The storehouse is anywhere the work of the Lord is going forth and producing results…the local church, a ministry, or wherever God and His Word is being honored.

Who is the devourer? The devourer is the devil, who only comes to steal, kill and destroy (John 10:10). God said that when you give, He will rebuke the devourer for your sake.

What does the word rebuke mean? It

means, "Stop it! That's enough!" When you bring your tithe and offerings unto the Lord, He says to the devil, "Stop it! That's enough!" He commands the devil to stop interfering in your affairs, and He continues to prosper you and to increase your seed for sowing (2 Corinthians 9:10-11).

Believing for the Miraculous or Settling for "Just Enough"

I love the story in Luke chapter 5 of when Jesus first showed Simon Peter His power and the miracle of multiplication. Jesus was walking along the shore of the Sea of Galilee when he saw Simon Peter and his men washing and mending their nets. Jesus went up to them and said, (I'm paraphrasing here): "Lend Me your boat, Simon Peter. I need it to preach from. Let

Me use your boat to bring healing to the people and to preach life and deliverance to them. And when I give it back to you, it won't come back in the same condition. Right now, your boat is empty. But when I give it back to you, it will be full."

Simon Peter obeyed the Lord and loaned Him his boat. Jesus taught the people from that boat and no doubt, performed miracles in their lives. And when He had finished, He said to Simon Peter, "Now, launch back out into the deep waters for a catch and let down your nets." Simon Peter replied, *"Master, we have toiled all night and caught nothing; nevertheless at Your word I will let down the net."*

You see, in those days, the fishermen didn't fish in the deep waters. Their boats were not strong enough to withstand the winds if a storm suddenly came up on them. The boat could capsize and they could all drown. So, they fished in the shallows. The thing was, the shallows is where only the small fish swam. The big fish were out in the deep waters. Jesus was encouraging him to use his faith, to step out into the deep waters, because that's where his miracle would be found.

I want to stop and make a point here… If you'll notice, in the scripture above, Jesus tells Simon Peter to let down his nets…*plural*. And his answer to Jesus was, "Yes, at Your word I will let down the net, "*singular*."

Jesus, however, had a *more-than-enough*, miracle catch waiting for Simon Peter. And when Jesus commanded all those fish to hit that one net, it broke! And when it broke, I'm thinking that Simon Peter might have looked astoundingly at Jesus and wondered why he had not fully obeyed the word of the Lord and let down more than one net! Because the haul of fish was so large, it filled both Simon Peter's and his partner's boats! They were so full, in fact, that they began to sink! I can imagine that Simon Peter might have been thinking, "Whew! I almost lost this net-breaking, boat-sinking miracle load of fish Jesus had for me."

You know, just like Simon Peter, so many people today don't fully listen to or obey God's Word. They tend to stay in the shallows where they feel safe, never examining whether their belief system is true or false, never exercising their faith. They'll put a little something in the offering plate, but don't want to commit to tithing—not understanding that they are limiting themselves and cutting themselves off from all God wants to do for them and in them.

Now, let me ask you, *Could you use a net-breaking, boat-sinking load of miracles in your life?*

Well, it can happen for you, too! However, according to God's Word, it isn't going to happen until you do something first. You must step out in faith and make the first move. You see, everything starts with faith. Faith is to be active and put to use; it doesn't just stand still (James 2:20). *Faith doesn't focus in on how big the problem is, but on how big our God is!* And how does faith come? Faith comes by hearing the Word of God (Romans 10:17). When we see it written in the Word of God… hear it… and believe it, *then*, we can begin to act on it, and faith is created.

God says in Hebrews 11:6 that it's our faith that pleases Him and that it's faith which He rewards. That's why I like to call Him an "if-then" God. *If* we will return to Him, *then* He will return to us. *If* we will do something first, in faith, *then* He will respond to our faith and do something on our behalf. *If* we will ask, seek and knock, *then* He will answer (Luke 11:9-10).

Simon Peter fell to his knees before Jesus and repented of his unbelief. The Lord responded, *"Don't be afraid. From now on, you will catch men."* And his life was never the same. Because he responded to and obeyed the word of the Lord, he received a life-change…an attitude change…a turnaround from fear to faith.

Friend, I just can't emphasize this message enough. I want it to get deep down into your spirit—**God WANTS you to prosper.** Just read these scriptures from the Bible…

> **GENESIS 39:21-23** *But the Lord was with Joseph and showed him mercy, and He gave him favor in the sight of the keeper of the prison. And the keeper of the prison committed to Joseph's hand all the prisoners who were in the prison; whatever they did there, it was his doing. The keeper of the prison did not look into anything that was under Joseph's authority, be-*

cause the Lord was with him; and whatever he did, the Lord made it prosper.

JOSHUA 1:5, 7-8 *No man shall be able to stand before you all the days of your life; as I was with Moses, so I will be with you. I will not leave you nor forsake you. Only be strong and very courageous, that you may observe to do according to all the law which Moses My servant commanded you; do not turn from it to the right hand or to the left, that you may prosper wherever you go. This Book of the Law shall not depart from your mouth, but you shall meditate in it day and night, that you may observe to do according to all that is written in it. For then you will make your way prosperous, and then you will have good success.*

1 KINGS 2:3 *And keep the charge of the Lord your God: to walk in His ways, to keep His statutes, His commandments, His* *judgments, and His testimonies, as it is written in the Law of Moses, that you may prosper in all that you do and wherever you turn.*

1CHRONICLES 22:13 *Then you will prosper, if you take care to fulfill the statutes and judgments with which the Lord charged Moses concerning Israel. Be strong and of good courage; do not fear nor be dismayed.*

2 CHRONICLES 20:20 *So they rose early in the morning and went out into the Wilderness of Tekoa; and as they went out, Jehoshaphat stood and said, "Hear me, O Judah and you inhabitants of Jerusalem: Believe in the Lord your God, and you shall be established; believe His prophets, and you shall prosper".*

2 CHRONICLES 26:5 *He sought God in the days of Zechariah, who had understanding in the visions of God; and as long as he sought the Lord, God made him prosper.*

JOB 36:11 *If they obey and serve Him, they shall spend their days in prosperity, and their years in pleasures.*

PSALM 1:1-3 *Blessed is the man who walks not in the counsel of the ungodly, nor stands in the path of sinners, nor sits in the seat of the scornful; But his delight is in the law of the Lord, and in His law, he meditates day and night. He shall be like a tree planted by the rivers of water, that brings forth its fruit in its season, whose leaf also shall not wither; and whatever he does shall prosper.*

When God's Word encourages you to give, it's not to take something from you. It's to get something to you. It's to get his *"good measure, pressed down, shaken together, and running over"* harvest of blessing into your life (Luke 6:38)!

Worthy or Unworthy— Who You Are in Christ

You might say, "Richard, I'm just not worthy to receive anything from God."

Who told you that? Where does it say that in the Bible? *It doesn't!*

You *are* worthy. You are unique and irreplaceable. There is no one else on the planet now, nor has there ever been anyone else just like you. You are the apple of God's eye. You are God's child.

And what loving parent would not give good things to their children? *If you then, being evil, know how to give good gifts to your children, how much more will your Father who is in heaven give good things to those who ask Him* (Matthew 7:11).

Key Points on Biblical Prosperity

The biblical principles of godly prosperity which I've outlined in this booklet are principles that I don't just talk about. I operate in them every day. They have transformed my ministry and my life…and I believe they can transform your life, too.

Let's review the key points on biblical prosperity which I've shared with you…

- The teaching of a "prosperity gospel" is not scriptural. The Word of God teaches "biblical prosperity."

- God wants you to prosper and to be in health. It's His highest wish for you.

- The way the world has taught us to prosper is to grab all we can, any way we can, and hold on to it at all costs. But in the long run, the world's way doesn't work!

- "Seed-faith" living puts you into position to receive all God has for you.

- Being in lack and having nothing in order to serve the Lord is not scriptural. God says in 2 Corinthians 9:6-12 that He will give seed to the sower and provide bread for food.

- Tithing is a biblical principle for today.

- God can only multiply or increase what we give to Him.

As I said before…being prosperous is *never* just about finances. Prospering in life is also about your time, your prayers, your smiles, your kind words and deeds and your pats on the back. It's all about our love for one another; doing unto others as we would have others do unto us. Only your imagination can limit the many ways in which you can give to others and to God.

God is a God of abundance, a more-than-enough God of multiplication. He wants you to not just get by in life… He wants you to *thrive* in Him.

And God is no respecter of persons; He doesn't discriminate. If God could do it for Abraham and Simon Peter and many others—not only in Bible times, but for so many all throughout history—He can do it for you… *today*!

I'd like to pray for you:

> *Friend, I pray that God would reveal to you through His Word what true Bible prosperity really means and how you can operate in it. I pray that you would make the decision today to live "from the inside out", obeying God and doing what He*

says. I pray that you would make a habit of renewing your mind to God's Word, casting down every negative thought and emotion that is contrary to His Word. I ask the Holy Spirit to bring Scripture to your remembrance which will help you to release your faith as never before and to believe for the abundant life Jesus came to give you. I pray in the authority of Jesus' name, and I rebuke the devil and command him to take his hands off of your life as I stand in faith with you for you to begin to thrive in Jesus and to experience His miracles. May you experience the joy of living a life of giving, of peaceful gratitude for God's goodness, and of the faithfulness of God's grace and provision…as you prosper in all things. In Jesus' name. Amen.

SCRIPTURES FOR FURTHER STUDY AND MEDITATION:

Genesis 28:4
Leviticus 26:3-5
Deuteronomy 8:18
Job 22:21
Psalm 37:4 & 105:8-10
Proverbs 3:9, 11:25 & 16:3
John 3:16-17
Acts 20:35
Romans 3:20-22, 4:17 & 8:1
Galatians 2:16 & 3:13-14
Ephesians 3:20-21
Philippians 4:19
Colossians 1:21
Hebrews 13:16
James 1:22
1 John 3:22

RICHARD ROBERTS

Richard Roberts, D. Min., is Chairman and Chief Executive Officer of the Oral Roberts Ministries. For over 30 years he has conducted healing services throughout America and around the world. Today his own international pastors conferences and healing services are marked by a tremendous move of the Spirit, with people often reporting a broad range of healing miracles—spiritually, physically, mentally, emotionally, and in other areas.

Other books by Richard Roberts: *Thrive –Eliminating Lack From Your Life, Your Road to a Better Life, The Return, He's A Healing Jesus,* and *Unstoppable Increase.*

For prayer,

call *The Abundant Life Prayer Group* at 918-495-7777, or contact us online at **www.oralroberts.com/prayer**.

RICHARD
ROBERTS
ORAL ROBERTS MINISTRIES